Overheard from Professor Binder's Former Students

I wish I would have just gone to Perry Binder University! Perry's enthusiasm was contagious and my cheeks would be sore from laughing after every class!
Kevin Walkup

I took Perry Binder's class my freshman year of college. Although it has now been over a decade, I remember his class as the one I most looked forward to because of his passion and knowledge of the subject. Today, I consider Perry a friend and his determination encouraged me to continue my education throughout grad school.
Sherlene Nelson

I will never forget coming back from surgery and the first thing Perry does is start the class on a welcome back chant for me. Kevin Clodfelter

Perry Binder was not only a Professor, but a Mentor. His classes were not about memorizing material, but taking it and applying to real-life scenarios.
Lizette Olaechea

Two essential lessons that Perry's class taught me are: important information is everywhere if we spend the time to look closer; and it's more meaningful to find humor in our daily lives than to live with fear, pessimism, or divisiveness. Those lessons go a long way toward finding happiness and reaching the success that we all imagine. Thomas Hodges

Binder is the Michael Jordan of te~~~~~ ~
Harlem Duru

Professor Binder's class kept us engaged the entire time. The best part was that he actually motivated his students, making us WANT to learn and succeed.
Anita Kathuria

Perry's class was more than just another class for me, it was a decision making catalyst, and had a huge impact on my future. His classes were the ones that I felt passionate about and never bored. Kevin Crayon

Perry provides a means of learning which applies to everyone in the classroom. There's a difference between being in class and wanting to be in class. Every lecture I attended, I can honestly say I wanted to be there.
Stephanie Beadle

To have shared a classroom with Perry was not only a learning experience, but a trajectory for life.
Vincent Suero

I appreciated Perry's commitment to helping my classmates and me go beyond our limited backgrounds and cultures and blossom into informed and caring professionals. Anthony Gerald

Professor Binder cares about his students and our world. He makes you think and ask yourself: How can I apply this to my reality and bring about justice?
Zyna Adams

Perry is so entertaining in the classroom that one often wonders why he hasn't taken up comedy as another career. Jennifer Flome

Anyone who has never made a mistake has not tried something new.
Albert Einstein

Seven years of college down the drain.
Bluto, in the movie *Animal House*

Dedication

This book is dedicated to any person who walks into a college classroom and dares to dream about a better today and tomorrow.

99 MOTIVATORS FOR COLLEGE SUCCESS

Motivational College Tips & Quotes on
Choosing a Career Path
Engaging in Class
Dealing with College Life

by
PERRY BINDER, J.D.

99Motivators.com

99 Motivators™ for College Success

Table of Contents

III. Motivators for Success in Adjusting to College Life

Quick Stories for College Life
- Know the consequences of no regrets.
- Figure out how to compensate for your weaknesses.
- In stressful moments, lean on your strengths.

Prologue

I never dreamed of being a college professor. Does anybody? When my third grade teacher asked us about our dream job, Molly said an astronaut; Evan, an actor. Perry: "Obtain a terminal degree and lecture on legal morasses."

Every college student wants a good laugh, I think. Humor can be found even in the most stressful situations. For example, I tell students that I can't offer legal advice. But that didn't stop "Steve" from calling me after class in a panic: "The judge gave me ten days for speeding; they're taking me away!"

So that night, I drove to the county jail, where the innkeeper ushered me into a tiny drab room facing glass. Steve appeared on the other side, looking weary and wearing an ugly orange jumpsuit. I never practiced criminal law, so I just put my hand up to the glass and spread my fingers apart because I saw that done on TV. Steve finally smiled and put his hand up to mine. He told me what happened, but all I could do was stare at our mitts and think: "Hey, this TV hand thing really works!"

While Steve's dilemma was no laughing matter, I use that story on the first day of class to set the tone for our semester: Understanding the law is serious business and applied unequally to young college students without counsel. But we will laugh and learn a lot together.

To me, humor for the college crowd mixes audience participation with storytelling about the bizarre world around us. Consider this recent headline: Man Pleads Guilty to DUI in Motorized Recliner. Who knew the law could be so funny?

But college isn't all about laughs. At times, many students feel anxiety and intimidation, mixed with a lost feeling in class, in career direction, and in life. That's where this book comes in.

99 Motivators™ for College Success offers my thoughts from over twenty years of college teaching. The Motivators are presented in bite-sized tips and quotes. Most are serious, some are quirky, and hopefully they are all constructive and motivational.

The book is divided into three sections:

I. Motivators for Success in Picking a Major or Career Path
II. Motivators for Success in the Classroom
III. Motivators for Success in Adjusting to College Life

Each Motivator contains space to jot down notes when a tip or quote resonates with you. At the end of each section, three "Takeaways" highlight the overarching Motivator themes, and then you are challenged to apply these concepts by writing three Personal Motivator Goals.

Three sections. Ninety nine Motivators. Nine Takeaways. Nine Personal Goals. This book will make you think hard about what you want out of your college experience and career in an easy to access format.

99 Motivators™ for College Success offers guidance on how to study for multiple choice exams, with sample questions and answers. Further, this book shows you how to write organized essays, by providing a sample essay exam question with model college and law school level responses.

99 Motivators™ for College Success is not only for people heading to college or already in college. It is also for the parents of students to better understand what's expected of children in college, and the pressures they face from professors, peers, and family members.

99 Motivators™ for College Success is for high school teachers and guidance counselors, and anyone else who facilitates the difficult transition process from high school to college for students. Finally, this book is for new and seasoned college professors seeking a fresh perspective on teaching.

If you are looking for a textbook on the A-Z steps for college and career success, then this book is not for you. Frankly, I am skeptical of books which promise a neat roadmap or a cure-all to the pressures of college or the work world. Instead, the value of *99 Motivators™ for College Success* is an opportunity for positive introspection on college and careers, with quick messages and jolts to your nervous system.

In *99 Motivators™ for College Success*, I am one part professor, one part college tour guide, and one part cheerleader. Let's get started on the path to college success, but first, my student Steve's verdict: I referred him to a criminal defense lawyer but Steve still spent three days in jail for speeding. It would've been zero if he had an attorney at the outset, which shows that maybe nothing is funny about the law after all!

Introduction

Someone once asked me how I can teach the same subjects year after year without getting bored. My response: Do you think that all recording artists get bored singing the same songs for the past twenty years? It may be the same song, but there's a different interpretation and a fluid audience each time. Likewise, my course material is similar from year to year. Meeting different students each time is the secret part of the equation which keeps things lively and exciting. While the structure is predictable, every semester has energy and a life of its own.

A professor's job is to keep things fresh and provocative, regardless of mood, subject, or student engagement. Naturally, my curious students ask me why I don't practice law anymore. The best answer I can come up with is an analogy from the movie, *Good Will Hunting*, when psychologist Sean Maguire (played by Robin Williams) is discussing personal relationships with his patient, Will. (Matt Damon)

Will just had a perfect first date with Skylar (Minnie Driver) and he tells Sean that he's never going to call her again. To which a surprised Sean inquires why. Will explains that the date was so perfect, that he didn't want to ruin that memory or image, and risk an imperfect second date.

The psychologist smiles and reminds his young patient that he's not so perfect himself, and neither is his recent date. The trick he says is to take a risk and discover whether you're perfect for each other.

Being a professor is not a perfect profession to some people, and I know I'm an imperfect teacher. But we're perfect for each other. I've learned, changed, grown, and gotten back more than I bargained for in many courtrooms and classrooms.

Today, I am refreshed and ready, but already messed up on the first day of the semester in front of 120 students. While I remembered to bring the syllabus, I forgot to bring their outline for the first unit. Maybe I have an overactive imagination or a hypersensitive ear, but I could've sworn I heard a student mutter under her breath: "This professor sucks!"

Now let's get motivated...

SUCCESS IN PICKING A MAJOR OR CAREER PATH

QUICK STORIES & MOTIVATORS 1-33

QUICK STORIES BEFORE PICKING A CAREER PATH

Never crush anyone's dreams.

When I was a little kid, I dreamed about playing professional basketball. In third grade, we had to write an essay on what we wanted to be when we grew up. I wrote that I wanted to be 6'10" and play in Madison Square Garden. When the teacher handed back my paper, she laughed out loud and said: "You can't do that!"

That was the first time someone had crushed my professional dream. The teacher may have been right about the 6'10" part, but this molder of young minds lacked the understanding of what negative reinforcement can do to little kids. She also lacked the understanding that height isn't everything for a basketball player. Teachers, especially in the impressionable K-12 years, are my personal heroes. Yet they need to be dream builders, not dream destroyers. It's healthy to discuss rational backup career plans, but why spoil youthful exuberance which could flower into the unexpected?

Postscript: When I was 25 years old, I got to play one-on-one with 7'4" center Mark Eaton of the Utah Jazz, that year's NBA Defensive Player of the Year. I'll leave the game results to your active imagination.

This story is the basis for Motivator #4

QUICK STORIES BEFORE PICKING A CAREER PATH

Do what you love but don't jeopardize anyone you love. Including yourself.

Recognize and assess the risks in every major decision you make, and how they affect those around you.

When I left the full-time practice of law to teach, I was single and had no children. Would I have made such a career transition if I had a spouse and two kids at the time? I'd like to think so because in the end, career satisfaction is one key to personal fulfillment. Some opportunities are rare and don't come around often. The difficult part is learning whether to jump at or pass on an adventure when your responsibilities require the support of those around you, and dictate a closer look at the risk and reward.

This story is the basis for Motivator #10

QUICK STORIES BEFORE PICKING A CAREER PATH

Figure out if you are a "structure" person or someone who can self-motivate at any given time.

Years ago, I briefly did freelance work full-time and found it difficult to motivate myself day in and day out. In that environment, you have to create a regimen and stick to it with discipline.

I like some structure in my daily routine, but not too much. Classes bring that framework to my work life. For me, just knowing that I need to be at a certain place on time brings me certainty, clarity, and anticipation.

This story is the basis for Motivator #12

#1

As a Freshman, it is not only okay to have no idea what to major in, it's also a sign of an open mind to the diverse menu that college has to offer. Choose classes which seem interesting to you rather than classes that parents or peers say you have to take immediately.

#2

Picking a career path boils down to a cost benefit analysis and a gut check. It is a game of reality versus passion, and hopefully you can start blazing a meaningful path in college. Check your gut instinct first and then assess your career options.

#3

Every career has an arc, and you are at the beginning of the curve. Don't be surprised if your career direction changes significantly a few times before and after you reach the peak.

Did You Know... The U.S. Bureau of Labor Statistics has not attempted to estimate the number of times people change careers in the course of their working lives. However, in September 2010, the Bureau found that from age 18 to age 44, individuals held an average of 11 jobs.

#4

Don't let anyone crush your dreams. However, the riskier your dream, the better your backup plan must be.

#5

If you have no backup plan in a career like acting, you not only need a fervent belief in your talent – you better <u>have</u> the talent to stay on a tight rope with no safety net beneath you. For more traditional fields, you will likely have an easier time transitioning into your dream job. (For example, Chemistry majors who didn't get accepted into a medical school can hopefully work for a year in that field and reapply to medical schools the following year.)

#6

There is a huge difference between a childhood dream and a dream job. If you dreamed of being a lawyer since the age of twelve, you better make sure you know exactly what attorneys do on a given twelve hour work day.

Did You Know... In a 2007 survey of 800 attorneys, only 55 percent reported being satisfied with their career.

#7

Make sure your dream job is not an avocation. (a hobby) An avocation is a vacation from a vocation, because the pay ranges from little to nothing.

#8

The most important thing for deciding on a major or career path is to get out of the classroom and into an internship which exposes you to the day-to-day ups and downs of that profession.
Learning by doing will give you a better appreciation of the job than learning through textbooks.

#9

Sometimes, doing the things your family or friends expect you to achieve in your career might be the wrong path for you.

#10

Do what you love but don't let your career choices jeopardize anyone you love. Including yourself. Translation: Take care of others but don't forget to take care of yourself, sometimes before others. Listen to our airline flight attendants: "Put your own oxygen mask on first before assisting others with their masks."

#11

Keeping a job is not just about your job skills. The more indispensible your interpersonal skills, the less vulnerable you are in a fluid job market. The best "team players" not only sacrifice for the team, they figure out how to deal with and work with less cooperative team members.

#12

Figure out if you want predictable structured working hours, or if you are motivated to work until the job gets done. Also, figure out whether you are willing to work during hours when most people play. (such as a real estate agent or someone in the hospitality field)

#13

Determine whether you are driven to be your own boss or if you crave the stability of a steady paycheck. Assess your personality traits and the risks inherent with both paths. (e.g., the risk of putting up your own money as your own boss versus the risk of losing a job in a company you work for)

#14

If you enjoy the challenge of daily rejection, a career in sales may be for you. If you thrive on daily conflict, become a litigation attorney.

#15

Pick a practical career path if your theme song is *Workin' for a Livin'*. Follow your dreams if your theme song is *Born to Run*.

Did You Know... The U.S. Bureau of Labor Statistics lists occupations with the largest job growth projected through the year 2018, starting with registered nurse.

#16

Choose a career path that closely mirrors not just your talents and ambitions, but also your internal compass. Criminal lawyers do not always get to pick the cases they work on. Federal and state public defenders often defend people who are guilty because everyone is entitled to representation. Are you able to ignore your compass when it points North, but the work assignment points South?

CAREER PATH MOTIVATOR

#17

"Life's under no obligation to give us what we expect."

Margaret Mitchell, author of *Gone with the Wind*

CAREER PATH MOTIVATOR

#18

"When you come to the fork in the road, take it."

Yogi Berra, former baseball player

#19

Persistence breeds success. Some of history's most famous people fell down and rose to greatness. When Michael Jordan was cut from his high school basketball team, he found even greater resolve to prove his worth.

#20

Keep in touch with your favorite professors after you complete their classes. Consider them a resource for career advice. Then when you graduate, teach them about what you've been learning after college.

#21

Rather than casually asking career advice from parents or other relatives, set up a time to interview them, with prepared general and specific questions. This approach will make them think more thoughtfully about their responses, and may reveal their personal career challenges and triumphs.

#22

Clean up your social media presence online – what's publicly available might not bode well for your future employment.

Did You Know... In 2011, the Federal Trade Commission approved the practice of employers conducting social media background checks going back seven years for job applicants.

#23

LinkedIn is the social media tool of choice for many professionals. Start a LinkedIn page and add every professional you meet at a networking function.

#24

"Networking" is not a dirty word. The beauty of social media is that you can network online with professionals to fit your comfort zone, if you are shy or intimidated when meeting professionals in person. However, face-to-face encounters are still the most effective means of networking, and an over-reliance on social networking tools may prove counterproductive in the long run.

#25

If a professor wants you to create a business concept and write a business plan, give him or her your second best idea. Hold onto your best idea for the real thing.

Did You Know... While it is true that the founder of FedEx pitched his business plan in a college class, it is not true that the professor declared the idea as "unworkable," or that the student received a "C" on the paper.

#26

If you create or own a unique product, consider licensing the non-exclusive rights to use the work over and over again to others. Ask Bill Gates if that model worked better than selling all rights to his original disk operating system. (DOS)

#27

Don't be afraid to ask others for help, as long as you are willing to do the same for others. Juniors and seniors are a great resource because they have recently walked in your shoes.

#28

Early in your college career, visit your university career services office with your resume. Career counselors can help you get started, especially if you have no idea where to begin. Most students overlook this valuable resource for career advice, job leads, and resume revisions.

#29

"By failing to prepare, you are preparing to fail. When you're finished changing, you're finished."

Ben Franklin

#30

No matter what your part-time jobs or summer jobs are, always be thinking about how those experiences will enhance your resume and work skills.

#31

Don't rely on luck or fate in your career. Professional success is about putting yourself in a position to create numerous opportunities.

#32

"If you don't know where you're going, you'll be lost when you get there."

Yogi Berra, former baseball player

#33

Over the course of your lifetime, there may only be a handful of impactful career opportunities. Assemble an inner circle team of advisors now, so you'll be able to act quickly to objectively assess the pluses and minuses of future opportunities.

TOP TAKEAWAYS: SUCCESS IN PICKING A MAJOR OR CAREER PATH

- The media shapes our impressions of what different careers are like. Research the benefits and challenges of your major and career path by interviewing people who work in that industry, and by securing an internship in that field.

- Keep an open mind when choosing a major or career path. Base these decisions on your likes, dislikes, personality, and work style, rather than on the expectations placed on you by family and peers.

- Don't let anyone crush your dreams. However, the riskier your dream, the better your backup plan must be.

PERSONAL MOTIVATOR GOALS

Based on Motivators 1-33, list three specific goals you will work on this year.

1.

2.

3.

SUCCESS IN THE CLASSROOM

QUICK STORIES
&
MOTIVATORS 34-66

QUICK STORIES FROM THE CLASSROOM

Learn at your own pace. You'll get there eventually.

My "welcome to college" moment occurred when I got a C-minus on my very first English paper. In a panic, I sought the advice of peers to figure out why that paper, which would've gotten me an" A" in high school, was a dud in Freshmen English.

As far back as I can remember, I was a slow learner when reaching new levels – middle school, high school, college, and law school. Once I got the hang of it though, I started to excel.

As a professor, I recognize that people don't get things right away, and that every class is an adjustment for students.

This story is the basis for Motivators #39 and #51

QUICK STORIES FROM THE CLASSROOM

Intelligence is wrapped in many packages.

As I sat in class during the first year of law school, I was confused at times when others raised their hands and offered wild legal theories. What I discovered after the fact is that classroom discussion leaders do not always perform as well on exams as the shy, silent student who doesn't utter a peep all semester.

Regardless, I don't equate good grades with intelligence. One psychologist, Robert Sternberg, identifies three types of intelligence in his Triarchic Model:

• Componential Intelligence – analytic, academic abilities to solve problems
• Experiential Intelligence – creativity and insight, the ability to invent, discover, and theorize
• Practical Intelligence – street smarts, ability to adapt to the environment

I once wrote a letter of recommendation for a student who received a "C" in my course because after many discussions outside of class, I recognized that he had the practical intelligence to succeed in his chosen profession.

This story is the basis for Motivator #41

QUICK STORIES FROM THE CLASSROOM

Distraction from learning is the key to learning.

The classroom gives me freedom to do things I couldn't do in a courtroom – be myself. In class, if I want to jump on a table or answer a student's ringing cell phone, it not only is acceptable, but is happily taken in by the class. I wonder if a judge would appreciate this behavior.

I like an atmosphere of expecting the unexpected. I actually welcome distractions and discovered that they help students retain material. When their minds are wandering, I need something to bring them back on track.

At the review for my first exam, students are typically very nervous, not really knowing what to expect on the test. To break the tension, I'll give my dry erase marker to a student sitting in the middle of the room. As I run back to the front of the classroom, I implore the student to stand up and wing the marker at my head! Some respectful students wouldn't think of committing a battery on their professor, until egged on by rowdy classmates.

I've been nailed only one time in all these years. And now let's get back to the exam review.

This story is the basis for Motivator #49

#34

The first day of class is the most important session because it sets the tone for the semester. Rather than grabbing a syllabus, tuning out, and leaving, expect more from yourself that day. You have the power to stay in or drop the class, so intently gauge the course relevance, workload, and potential deliverables.

#35

Make a friend on the first day of class so you can swap class notes when needed. Even if the notes stink, you've made a new friend.

#36

Texting in class is better than talking to your neighbor. It's more discreet and less distracting to the professor and students around you.

#37

Think twice before you post something about classes on Facebook or Twitter. It is unwise to "Tweet" ugly thoughts, especially under the hash tag "#BoredinClass." Your professors may actually be active on social networks.

#38

Your professors are rooting for you to succeed. When you fail, they fail.

#39

Learn at your own pace because there's no such thing as quick learners or slow learners - just learners. If you have difficulties adjusting to the rigors of college, check out your university learning center, which provides student support in research, writing, study techniques, and public speaking.

#40

"The beautiful thing about learning is that no one can take it away from you."

BB King, Blues Guitarist

#41

Intelligence is wrapped in many packages. "Book smarts" is only one measure, but you still need to strive for good grades. The best way to figure out how to study is to attend class and observe what topics are important to professors. Those subjects usually wind up on their exams.

#42

We are all procrastinators of some sort. The best procrastination killer is to involve others in your task. It's much easier to let yourself down than to let others down. Use team synergy to get your piece of the puzzle done quicker.

#43

Some people shine with a raised hand in class. Some students know the answer but are too shy to raise a hand. Some just zone out in class. Two out of three ain't bad.

#44

Your attention span in class is like shooting basketball free throws. At times you can go 10 for 10, 5 for 10, or 0 for 10. Set your feet, take a deep breath, dribble twice. Refocus. Release. Follow through.

#45

Computer spell check is not the same as proofreading. My mother always said "If you don't know a word, look it up." She never did like my reply: "But I don't know how to spell it!"

#46

Expect the unexpected in class from your professors. They may surprise you with an insight or lesson that you won't be able to look up in a textbook or online. Referencing it later on in an essay exam or paper will be gratifying to the professor.

#47

A college class is like a Hollywood screenplay, with plot points and escalating conflicts along the way. Your professor may be the writer, director, and critic, but you are the lead actor and protagonist who must navigate the obstacles and perform well on each test thrown at you.

#48

If your professor offers extra credit projects, do them! "Lack of time" is not a good excuse if given ample time to complete the task. "Trying to get a good grade on my own" is a noble reason, but there is no shame in accepting alternative ways to succeed.

#49

If you study for three hours straight, make sure you take a lot of short study breaks. Distraction from learning is the key to retaining what you've learned.

#50

Don't get shook up by a shaky first semester. College is a marathon, not a sprint, and you're just warming up.

#51

What worked in high school may not work in college. If you get a C on your first Freshman English paper, it's time to be proactive rather than passive. To get back on track, don't be afraid to talk with your professors, fellow students, and professionals at your university learning center.

#52

Laughter is the best medicine for an exceptionally lousy day. Rather than brooding about a bad exam grade, watch a good comedy and give yourself a good belly laugh. But you better get fired up for the next day.

#53

Sometimes a final course grade does not reflect your effort or what you've actually learned. True learning occurs regardless of grades when a class refines your skill sets, your thought processes, or both. It is nice to get that good grade though!

#54

Approach class like you should approach life: No matter how boring or stressful the day is, find some fun in learning something new.

#55

When developing a study schedule, figure out if you are a structure person or someone who can self-motivate at any given time. Structure people must develop and stick to a firm study schedule. Self-motivators who happen to be procrastinators need to consider working like structure people.

#56

You may be intimidated by your professor's knowledge, but that's a function of your experience, not your abilities. Have confidence in your capacity to learn and you may surprise yourself on what you are capable of accomplishing in class.

#57

Your professors may be subject matter experts, but that doesn't mean their opinions are always right. If you disagree, back up your opinions with solid facts.

#58

Listen to the ideas of others, interpret them, and draw your own conclusions.

#59

"It is the mark of an educated mind to be able to entertain a thought without accepting it."

Aristotle

#60

Deadline pressure facilitates efficient work. For lengthy term papers, create hard deadlines for your research, first draft, second draft, and completed draft.

#61

View your writing as a craft. It took Harper Lee over two years to write *To Kill a Mockingbird*. When you proofread, edit, and restructure your term papers, do you take two seconds, two minutes, or two hours? Or hopefully much longer?

Remember that "the best writing is rewriting."

E.B. White, author of *The Elements of Style*

#62

When finals week rolls around and there's nothing left in your gas tank, you've got no choice but to shift your gear into overdrive and ride those fumes to the finish line. But throughout the following semester, continually review class material, so you've got more than enough fuel at the finish.

#63

Ask your professors how they would study for their own exams.

#64

Prepare flashcards for straightforward multiple choice exam questions. Make a flashcard for each term or concept discussed in class. Put the term on the front, with a definition and example applying the term on the back.

See Appendix A; How to Study for Straightforward Multiple Choice Questions

#65

For "application" multiple choice questions (questions which go beyond memorization and make you apply what you've learned), talk the material out with a classmate. A well written college exam question will make you think critically about the course material.

See Appendix B; How to Approach "Application" Multiple Choice Questions

#66

On essay exams, ask your professor beforehand if you can write answers in an "essay outline" format. Except on open-ended questions, they are usually looking for some specific responses, so underline the key terms. This method will draw professors to your most important points in an organized and efficient manner. It will also make professors happy because the essay will be easier to grade!

For an example of an "essay outline" format, see Appendix C: How to Write a College Essay Exam Answer

TOP TAKEAWAYS: SUCCESS IN THE COLLEGE CLASSROOM

- Seek out a friend in every class you take, so you can share lecture notes and maybe even study together.

- Develop and stick to a firm studying schedule. Procrastinators often claim to be self-motivators and need to consider working like structure people.

- Your professors are rooting for you to succeed. Ask them how they would study for their own exams. Request practice quizzes, with the answers explained in class.

PERSONAL MOTIVATOR GOALS

Based on Motivators 34-66, list three specific goals you will work on this year.

1.

2.

3.

SUCCESS IN ADJUSTING TO COLLEGE LIFE

QUICKS STORIES

&

MOTIVATORS 67-99

QUICK STORIES FOR COLLEGE LIFE

Know the consequences of no regrets.

I had a student who said there was a "pie in the sky" casting call for some production, but it meant getting in line and waiting for hours at a downtown hotel. And missing my class.

I simply told her that she could go, but was responsible for getting class notes from a fellow student. I believe in going after opportunities, even when it means sometimes doing the irresponsible thing, like telling a professor that you need to ditch class for a pipe dream of a chance at something big.

I learned that lesson as a law student, when I was clerking at the U.S. Attorney's Office. A movie was being filmed downtown starring Robert Redford, and they needed extras to fill up an old minor league baseball stadium. Instead of playing on green grass, I did the responsible thing by going to work that day.

Years later, every time I see *The Natural*, I say to myself: "If only I called in sick that day." Thankfully, this is a minor regret. It serves as a lesson to me about risk taking and understanding the consequences. Be a risk taker in your college life, but know where to draw the foul line.

This story is the basis for Motivator #73

QUICK STORIES FOR COLLEGE LIFE

Figure out how to compensate for your weaknesses.

One of my glaring weaknesses as a professor is an inability to remember student names or recognize their faces outside of class. One time in class, a student walked up to me and said: "I saw you on campus yesterday, and you didn't even say 'hi.' That was rude!" I desperately tried to explain that names and faces are hard for me to recall in a class with 120 students.

So now, when I walk around a campus of 30,000 students, I'm compelled to wave hello to everyone I make contact with. "Hi, how goes it?!" Four out of five of them are looking at me, like: "Do I know you?" But that fifth person, the one I should know, appreciates the hello.

So now I'm walking, smiling, waving, and babbling. All over campus.

This story is the basis for Motivator #82

QUICK STORIES FOR COLLEGE LIFE

In stressful moments, lean on your strengths.

I learned this lesson on day one of the first class I ever taught, *Introduction to American Government*.

I thought that we should start class at the very beginning of the text, with a discussion of the Founding Fathers and the Federalist Papers. As I was speaking, I repeatedly said to myself: "You don't know anything about this topic beyond what you read last night." After forty five minutes of panic, sweat, and utter confusion, we took a ten minute break. In that time, I decided to go straight to the Bill of Rights, a topic of strength. The rest of the session thankfully went more smoothly.

This story is the basis for Motivator #82

#67

Psychologists say that past behavior is the best predictor of future behavior. Hogwash. You can learn from the past, live in the present, and work on your future.

#68

Scientific research reveals that the brain's impulse mechanism is not fully developed until around the age of 25. If you do something incredibly stupid or irrational and don't know why, at least science is on your side.

#69

Once you've made it to college, you've got adult decisions to make, like picking a career path. Stop letting people drive your decision-making process, even if they are footing your bills. Approach problems and decisions from the vantage point of a young adult.

#70

Live up to and learn to exceed your own expectations, not those imposed on you by family, peers, or cultural images from television and the movies.

#71

Stay true to the core of who you are. Don't buy into the commonly held belief that the older you get, the more you need to compromise your ethics and ideals.

#72

Try to be more of a "touch wet paint" person. Curiosity is more interesting than wondering if the day's paint is wet or dry.

#73

Live life with no regrets but understand the consequences of your decisions. Your professors should understand that you need to miss class to attend a job interview. However, you will still be responsible for getting class notes and making up any required work.

#74

The media wrongly labels the youth of every generation like an X or Y or Z. However, college students bring energy and a common message of hope to the table. Speak your mind when you have something important to say, however misguided others may think you are.

#75

Great words are far greater than the person who wrote them or uttered them. The truer measure of success is putting those words into action.

#76

Being a good listener is more important than being a good talker. The listener learns to read people and situations. The talker is thinking about what to say next.

#77

Before judging people, be willing to walk in their shoes for a day.

#78

Success is all about how you feel at the end of the day – not what's in your wallet or in the bank.

#79

In college life, don't focus on the problems. Focus on the solution to problems.

#80

If you are away from home for the first time, bring three loads of laundry back on your first trip home. On future trips, you'll know you've adjusted to college life when you stop bringing home dirty laundry.

#81

Examine your limits of love in college. When you hear the magic but scary words "If you love me," at what point do you lay low in the weeds?

a. If you love me, you'll do the laundry tonight.

b. If you love me, you'll visit my mom this weekend.

c. If you love me, you'll help me cheat on that exam.

d. If you love me, you'll help me bury that corpse stashed in my dorm room.

#82

In stressful moments, learn to lean on your strengths. Then, figure out how to compensate for your weaknesses.

#83

Try to always stay positive: "I'd rather spend 100% of the time on the 90% that's good – than 100% on the 10% that's not so good."

Bud Greenspan, Olympic filmmaker

#84

Success is about you and your friends achieving goals. Your motto should not be "Why not me?" Rather, make it "Why not us, why not me?"

#85

"Remember, nobody wins unless everybody wins."

Bruce Springsteen, Rock musician

#86

"Achieving success alone and at others' expense will get lonely."

Sarah Homsi, Professor Binder's former student

#87

Join a student organization in your Freshman year and volunteer to do everything. You will be noticed, stand out, and eventually position yourself to run that organization. You will then have something unique to put on your resume.

#88

In college – like high school – you face many "fitting in" tests. The good news is that college offers many more choices to join student organizations which match your interests, and thus a greater opportunity to fit in quicker with others.

#89

Advice for kids: Look both ways when crossing the street and don't talk to strangers. Advice for you: Look both ways when talking to strangers.

#90

Advice for kids: We work before we play but always try to have fun. Advice for you: We work before we play but always try to have fun.

#91

Always be yourself in social settings, but borrow conversational techniques from others. As an example, watch the *Reservoir Dogs* movie scene which starts: "Look man, an undercover cop got to be Marlon Brando, right? ... You got to be naturalistic."

#92

Greed for knowledge and the pursuit of truth is good.

#93

Do not be impressed with anyone's titles, degrees, or experience — only their actions and reactions to you and others are what should matter.

#94

Empathy towards others is not a weakness. It is a quality of maturity, strength, and clarity.

#95

Take a Personal Finance course. Even philosophy majors can't debate the meaning of a balanced checkbook.

#96

Take a law or philosophy course if you seek different perspectives on justice. "Justice is conscience, not a personal conscience but the conscience of the whole of humanity."

Alexander Solzhenitsyn, author of *The Gulag Archipelago*, in a letter written in October 1967

#97

Recommend to others the books which move you. Ask them to do the same for you.

See Appendix E; Books that Motivate Professor Binder

#98

Here's proof that there are many avenues to happiness. Preliminary findings in a research study on Happiness reveals that the most happiness-inducing activities in descending order are: Intimacy; Sports/running/exercise; Attending theater/dance/concert; Singing/performing; Attending an exhibition/museum/library; Hobbies/arts/crafts.

#99

If possible, study abroad for a summer or semester. You'll learn more about life and yourself than you will at your home institution.

TOP TAKEAWAYS: SUCCESS IN ADJUSTING TO COLLEGE LIFE

- Every college has many social and career-focused organizations. Figure out which groups to participate in for fun and for your future.

- Learn what your strengths are and how to use them in stressful situations. You already know what your weaknesses are – now figure out how to compensate for them.

- Live life with no regrets but understand the consequences of your decisions, whether they relate to classes, your future, or personal matters.

PERSONAL MOTIVATOR GOALS

Based on Motivators 67-99, list three specific goals you will work on this year.

1.

2.

3.

Read the Contract! (and other Lessons)

One of my former students thought she bought a new car, only to discover that she actually had leased the vehicle. Though the dealer told her she purchased the car, she realized this statement was inaccurate when she received her payment booklet in the mail. On the contract she signed but never read, the word "Lease" appeared at the top, rather than "Finance Agreement" or "Security Agreement." I sent her right back to the dealer that day, armed with all sorts of ethical and legal arguments.

Luckily, the dealer tore up the lease and replaced it with a finance agreement at the same payment terms. I don't know if she struck a good deal, but you can't make it that easy for merchants to take you down. Rule #1: At least read the title of the contract!

Class hypothetical: Sally went into a car dealer one evening and signed a contract to purchase a truck. When she expressed her hesitancy to sign the contract, the dealer closed the deal by saying to her: "Drive the truck around for a week; if you still have doubts, come back and we'll cancel the deal." Sally had no witnesses to this statement. She went back to the dealer the next morning, regretting the amount of money that the truck will cost. Of course, the dealer said that she couldn't get out of the contract.

The dealer gets to stand on a standard clause in the contract which would exclude the statement made by the dealer to the buyer. However, the statement was still a misrepresentation of fact - leading to several legal claims including fraud. But where is our witness? How can we prove this in court? Unless the written agreement states that you have a certain number of days to cancel the contract, you need to assume that you cannot get out of it. A consumer in this scenario should immediately turn to state and federal consumer statutes to see if there are any remedies.

Does Sally have leverage in this case to get out of the deal? Probably not, but what could she do? When trapped in a bad deal, I believe in creating leverage.

Leverage in this situation is obviously created when armed with an attorney. However, not everyone has that luxury. The next step is to get a consumer advocate working for you, and as a last resort, taking your case to the media. The dealer might want to avoid the bad publicity and work it out. Otherwise, I'm afraid that Sally will have little or no recourse.

Note: Sally better be correct in any assertion to the media, because this kind of action can lead to a slander lawsuit by the dealer.

Leverage is the determining factor for writing a good contract that the other side will sign. If the other side "needs the deal" more than we do, we'll have leverage in the negotiations. If there is ever a contract dispute, hopefully the language we negotiate will back us up. Leverage comes in many forms, and it usually comes down to money.

A cynical comment – Some people believe that contracts are made to be broken. Just because parties signed on the dotted line, it doesn't mean all is well. If business people sign a bad deal and are losing money, they might try to renegotiate the terms of the deal. If the other side does not agree to these terms, some people will consider breaching the contract to force a more reasonable arrangement. If that person has a bigger "war chest" (more money) than the person wishing to enforce the deal, that translates into leverage and possibly a favorable deal.

Takeaway #1: If you don't know what you're doing in a business transaction, take someone with you who does.

Takeaway #2: Do not sign a contract without fully knowing the consequences of your actions.

Takeaway #3: Take a law and ethics class at some point in your college career!

A Final Note on Leverage in Negotiations

In a good negotiation, the goal is not to figuratively beat the other side into submission. If the leverage is clearly on your side, I guess you have the opportunity to do so, but this tact will cause resentment down the road if you have dealings with the same person. When leverage is on an equal playing field, the goal for getting a deal done should be to get both sides what they want. When you benefit from a deal and the other side feels good about it, you may have begun a long term business relationship which could bear even greater fruit.

An extreme analogy to illustrate this point is the Cuban Missile Crisis. In 1962, the world was on the brink of nuclear war when Soviet General Secretary Nikita Khrushchev authorized the building of missile bases in Cuba, just off U.S. shores. When President Kennedy ordered a blockade of Soviet ships carrying weapons to Cuba, the leaders conducted secret ongoing negotiations. Eventually the Soviets relented, withdrawing the weapons and dismantling the missile bases. Kennedy gained instant respect worldwide, while Khrushchev was embarrassed by his alleged weakness.

Unknown at the time though was that the deal hinged on the United States agreeing to dismantle its own missile base in Turkey, along the Soviet Union's border.

Had Khrushchev been able to claim an immediate victory for the Turkey deal, he could've "saved face" in the crisis aftermath, and possibly even be viewed as a hero to his country. Instead, he was out of office within two years, and relations between the two powers remained tense for decades.

Business deals should be a little easier to manage than superpower negotiations. Simply put, if you make the other side look like heroes to the people who hold them accountable, they are more likely to do business with you again.

Graduation

When I participate in graduation ceremonies, I often imagine delivering my own speech to the graduates, as if I were the commencement speaker:

Good morning chancellor, president, deans, faculty members, staff, students, friends, and family members. And to the graduates:

Every one of you is special.
Every one of you is a productive member of society.
Every one of you is what inspires ME - because...
Every one of you has a story to tell.
I just wish I had the time to hear every one of them, and to be there as your career paths unfold.

You have already accomplished a huge milestone on that journey. The biggest step though was just showing up. That's it. The secret most people don't get until it's too late. Just showing up as young freshmen was a threshold event. Trying something which may be hard for the first time. Experiencing new things, even if it's unknown whether the objective is attainable.

To me, the greatest barriers to success, however you define that, are a fear of the unknown, a fear of change, and a fear of failure.

But you need a game plan, and hopefully you can lean a little on what you learned in school to figure out that route. No matter what you do in life, you always will have your education.

I hope you made some lifelong friends here. Frankly, I learned more about life from my peers than from my professors. And I hope you got more than knowledge from your profs because you can get that from a book. I'm hoping you gained insight on whatever subject, and then stamped your own original perspective on how to resolve issues and solve problems.

Many times the things you do won't work. And you will fail at some things you try. That's just a fact of life. Abraham Lincoln once said: "My great concern is not whether you have failed, but whether you are content with your failure."

And you will make mistakes. A lot of them! Both in your careers and your lives. That's just another fact of life. But that's okay. The trick is figuring out how to deal with setbacks. Your family and friends will always be there for you. And your education will continually serve as a foundation to get you back on track.

Franklin D. Roosevelt said: "We are not prisoners of fate, but only prisoners of our own minds." Graduates, each of you must unlock your mind and blaze a path built on reason and purpose. Life is too short to spend it bouncing around like a random and aimless ball in a game of Pong.® And whether you are 20, 30, 40, 50, 60, 70, or 80 years young, it is never too late to test the boundaries of your dreams.

Finally, I want all of you gathered in front of me to please lose the title of "former" student, because you will be my students for many years to come. And I expect in return that I can become *your* student, as I learn about your professional successes, trials, and tribulations.

Every one of you is special.
Every one of you is a productive member of society.
Every one of you is what inspires me – because...
Every one of you has a story to tell.

What will your next journey be?

Epilogue

L.I.G.H.T. B.U.L.B. Moments for New Professors and Teachers

In the Introduction to this book, I wrote:

Being a professor is not a perfect profession to some people, and I know I'm an imperfect teacher. But we're perfect for each other. I've learned, changed, grown, and gotten back more than I bargained for in many courtrooms and classrooms. Today, I am refreshed and ready, but already messed up on the first day of the semester in front of 120 students. While I remembered to bring the syllabus, I forgot to bring their outline for the first unit. Maybe I have an overactive imagination or a hypersensitive ear, but I could've sworn I heard a student mutter under her breath: "This professor sucks!"

Aside from these embarrassing classroom moments that all professors and teachers experience, I try to live up to my own expectations in class through an acronym:

Perry's L.I.G.H.T. B.U.L.B. Moments for New Professors and Teachers

L. isten to all learners
I. nspire them with real world discussions
G. ive hope to everyone
H. eap compliments on students for quality work
T. each to your strengths

B. e available at all times, whether in person or electronically
U. nderstand that students may lack your life experience or knowledge
L. earn from your learners
B. e willing to walk in your students' shoes

Have you found your light bulb moment?

Appendix A

How to Study for Straightforward Multiple Choice Questions

Prepare flashcards for straightforward multiple choice exam questions. Make a flashcard for each term or concept discussed in class. Put the term on the front, with a definition and example applying the term on the back. **(Motivator #64)**

On the front of the index card:
DUTY TO TRESPASSERS

On the back:
IN GENERAL, HOMEOWNERS MAY BE LIABLE FOR CREATING DANGEROUS INSTRUMENTALITIES ON THEIR PROPERTY. EXAMPLE: JANE SURROUNDS HER HOME WITH A MOTE FILLED WITH WATER AND ALLIGATORS TO MAKE SURE TOM STAYS OFF THAT FRESHLY CUT LAWN.

Make sure to study the flashcards in reverse. (look at the back of the card to see if you can identify the term on the front)

Sample Straightforward
Multiple Choice Question

Harold Homeowner didn't like having the neighborhood teenagers walk across his yard every night. So he dug a huge hole on his lawn, along the path the teens usually take. Then he placed a bear trap at the bottom of the hole and cleverly covered it with small branches and leaves. One night while walking across Harold's property, Tim fell in, got caught in the bear trap, and was seriously injured. The next morning, Harold went out for the newspaper and to see what he'd caught. Tim screamed: "My leg. I'm hurt!" In Tim's lawsuit for injuries, Harold will likely:

a. win because Tim was a trespasser and landowners owe no duty to trespassers. Harold could even surround his home with a mote filled with water and alligators to make sure Tim stays off his freshly cut lawn.

b. lose because landowners owe a duty to keep the premises free from unreasonable dangers they create for trespassers.

I know which answer you'd like to pick. Choose the other one for exam purposes.

Appendix B

How to Approach "Application" Multiple Choice Questions

For "application" multiple choice questions (questions which go beyond memorization and make you apply what you've learned), talk the material out with a classmate. A well written college exam question will make you think critically about the course material. **(Motivator #65)**

Answering the question below requires a three step thought process:

-   Understanding the legal concept of "comparative negligence," explained below

-   Using common sense in a simple mathematical calculation

-   Knowing to apply a state rule for comparative negligence

Sample "Application"
Multiple Choice Question

This morning on the way to his exam at a university in the state of Georgia, Marcel purchased coffee at the drive-through window of a local burger establishment. With the car stopped, he placed the cup between his knees and opened the lid to add cream. Accidentally, he knocked the contents of the cup onto his lap, and hot coffee soaked through his sweat pants. He screamed: "Help me, I'm burning, and I've got a test in 20 minutes!" After completing his exam, Marcel headed straight to the hospital, where doctors treated his third degree burns. He then sued the burger joint for failing to warn him that extremely hot coffee can rip through flesh. A jury awarded Marcel $100,000 in damages, but also found him to be 75% responsible and the defendant 25% responsible for the accident. How much money would Marcel be permitted to recover if the defendant does not appeal this verdict?

a. $100,000
b. $75,000
c. $25,000
d. $0

If you chose letter "c," then you understand the legal concept of comparative negligence. In most states, a plaintiff's award is reduced by the percentage of fault assigned by the jury for an accident. However, in some states, if a plaintiff is found to be 50% or more responsible, then that plaintiff would recover nothing from the $100,000 verdict. Thus, the correct response for those states would be letter "d." Moral of the story: Know your state laws!

Appendix C
How to Write a College Essay Exam Answer

On essay exams, ask your professor if you can write answers in an "essay outline" format. Except on open-ended questions, professors are usually looking for some specific responses, so underline the key terms. This method will draw professors to your most important points in an organized and efficient manner. It will also make professors happy because the essay will be easier to grade! **(Motivator #66)**

Sample Essay Exam Question

Assume that everyone in our class is a cast member (the "Cast") of a new reality television show, Legal Environment 101, set in a huge mansion where the Cast gets to live, sleep, and study. The producers of the show place $1,000,000 in the Cast bank account, to spend at its discretion on house-related needs. At the first house meeting, the Cast agrees that everyone lives like slobs, so it collectively decides to seek out the best home cleaner in the business.

The Cast interviews Bob the Cleaner, who earns $1,000,000/year cleaning several messy mansions nearby. Bob and the Cast sign an exclusive contract where Bob is to clean the Cast's house five days/week for one full year. Thereafter, Bob informs his current clients that he can't clean their homes because of this contract. The Cast puts a provision in the contract stating that Bob must work the full year to receive the money, otherwise he receives no compensation. Bob agrees to this stipulation, though the Cast does not explain its reason in the contract.

Bob gets to work right away, with a mop, bucket, and gritty determination. For the next six months, Bob does a stellar job. In fact, several house members have raved about Bob on Facebook, and not one house member has registered a complaint about Bob's work. The next day, Bob requests a house meeting with the Cast. With cameras rolling, Bob looks at everyone and in a dramatic moment of television history states: "You are all a bunch of slobs and I quit today. You owe me $500,000 right now."

Discuss all legal issues involved and conclude whether Bob would win if he filed a Complaint against the Cast and producers of Legal Environment 101.

Sample College Level Essay Answer

Plaintiff, Bob, may have actions at law and in "equity." He will sue both the Cast and producers of Legal Environment 101, as detailed below. In the <u>Discovery</u> process of the lawsuit, he might find more information as to the liability of the parties.

- An <u>Action at Law</u> is a cause of action which derives from traditional British common law, where parties usually may seek a remedy before a judge or jury.
- <u>Equity Actions</u> were derived from England's Chancery courts, and serve to remedy or supplement the limitations of common law. In most cases, only a judge may hear Equity claims with concepts of fairness.

Plaintiff, Bob's Possible Causes of Action v. The Cast and Producers ("Defendants")

A. Breach of Contract (Action at Law)
   - Bob will file a Breach of Contract claim. However, the face of the contract says that he must work one year to collect $1,000,000, so he likely would lose this claim.
B. Quantum Meruit (Equity)
   - If Bob cannot recover for Breach of Contract, he may ask the judge for the value of his services. (Quantum Meruit) By showing the judge that he worked for six months, he will sue "off the contract" and argue that his services are worth half of $1,000,000, or $500,000. In support of his claim, he can present earnings for previous years. In addition, he can introduce evidence that none of the Cast members were dissatisfied with his services and in fact, many of them gave rave reviews of his work on Facebook.
C. Promissory Estoppel (Equity)
   - Promissory Estoppel is when someone relies on a promise and is harmed. In reliance on the Cast's promise, Bob signed an exclusive contract and had to give up his cleaning appointments with other clients. If Bob is now unable to regain his old business clients, he may be able to argue that his reliance on the exclusive contract led to lost income.

Possible Defense for the Cast/Producers

The One Year Stipulation
- The Defendants will assert that the one year stipulation is unambiguous and is a condition precedent to the contract. (something a party is supposed to do as stated in the contract before something else can occur) Neither the fact pattern nor the contract provides further information on why the one year clause was inserted into the contract.

Conclusions

1- Bob will likely lose his Breach of Contract claim, but should prevail on his Quantum Meruit claim. (with the amount of damages determined by the judge)
2- The fact pattern does not provide enough information to assess the merits of the Equity claim for Promissory Estoppel, or for the Defendants' One Year Stipulation defense.

Appendix D

Bonus: How to Write a
Law School Essay Exam Answer

Sample Essay Exam Question
Same exam question as Appendix C, but with a more detailed essay answer

Assume that everyone in our class is a cast member (the "Cast") of a new reality television show, Legal Environment 101, set in a huge mansion where the Cast gets to live, sleep, and study. The producers of the show place $1,000,000 in the Cast bank account, to spend at its discretion on house-related needs. At the first house meeting, the Cast agrees that everyone lives like slobs, so it collectively decides to seek out the best home cleaner in the business.

The Cast interviews Bob the Cleaner, who earns $1,000,000/year cleaning several messy mansions nearby. Bob and the Cast sign an exclusive contract where Bob is to clean the Cast's house five days/week for one full year. (Bob informs his current clients that he can't clean their homes because of this contract) The Cast puts a provision in the contract stating that Bob must work the full year to receive the money, otherwise he receives no compensation. Bob agrees to this stipulation, though the Cast does not explain its reason in the contract.

Bob gets to work right away, with a mop, bucket, and gritty determination. For the next six months, Bob does a stellar job. In fact, several house members have raved about Bob on Facebook, and not one house member has registered a complaint about Bob's work. The next day, Bob requests a house meeting with the Cast. With cameras rolling, Bob looks at everyone and in a dramatic moment of television history states: "You are all a bunch of slobs and I quit today. You owe me $500,000 right now."

Discuss all legal issues involved and conclude whether Bob would win if he filed a Complaint against the Cast and producers of Legal Environment 101.

Sample Law School Level Essay Answer

Plaintiff, Bob, may have actions at law and in "equity." He will sue both the Cast and producers of Legal Environment 101, as detailed below. (In the Discovery process of the lawsuit, he might find more information as to the liability of the parties)

- An Action at Law is a cause of action which derives from traditional British common law, where parties usually may seek a remedy before a judge or jury.
- Equity actions were derived from England's Chancery courts, and serve to remedy or supplement the limitations of common law with concepts of fairness. In most cases, only a judge may hear Equity claims.

Plaintiff, Bob's Possible Causes of Action v. The Cast and Producers ("Defendants")

A. Breach of Contract (Action at Law)
   - Bob will file a Breach of Contract claim. However, the face of the contract says that he must work one year to collect $1,000,000, so he likely would lose this claim.

B. Quantum Meruit (Equity)
   - If Bob cannot recover for Breach of Contract, he may ask the judge for the value of his services. (Quantum Meruit) By showing the judge that he worked for six months, he will sue "off the contract" and argue that his services are worth half of $1,000,000, or $500,000. In support of his claim, he can present earnings for previous years. In addition, he can introduce evidence that none of the Cast members were dissatisfied with his services and in fact, many of them gave rave reviews of his work on Facebook.

C. Promissory Estoppel (Equity)
   - Promissory Estoppel is when someone relies on a promise and is harmed. In reliance on the Cast's promise, Bob signed an exclusive contract and had to give up his cleaning appointments with other clients. If Bob is now unable to regain his old business clients, he may be able to argue that his reliance on the exclusive contract led to lost income.

Possible Defenses and Options for the Cast/Producers

A. Special Skills
- The Defendants may argue that Bob is the only person in the entire state with the skills necessary to complete the contract. Thus they will be damaged if they are unable to find a suitable replacement.
  o If so, they may be able to file a counterclaim for damages incurred by not being able to replace Bob.
  o The Defendants would not likely be able to force Bob to complete the contract even if his skills are unique.
    ▪ Specific Performance (Equity) is a request to a judge to make another party perform pursuant to the terms of a contract. However, the courts generally frown upon this remedy in personal service contracts.
- These points may be moot, since neither the fact pattern nor the contract indicates that Bob had special skills.

B. The One Year Stipulation
- The Defendants will assert that the one year stipulation is unambiguous and is a condition precedent to the contract. (something a party is supposed to do as stated in the contract before something else can occur) Neither the fact pattern nor the contract provides further information on why the one year clause was inserted into the contract.

- o <u>Parol Evidence Rule</u>
  - If this matter made it to trial, the Defendants would argue that the one year stipulation is clearly written. The parol evidence rule states <u>that if a contract is unambiguous, then oral testimony or prior contract drafts are not permitted into evidence to contradict the final draft</u>.
- C. <u>Declaratory Judgment</u> (Equity)
  - Before Bob files his Complaint, the Cast and Producers could file a Complaint merely <u>seeking a judge's interpretation of the contract</u>. (Declaratory Judgment) This could be done as a preemptive move to have the contract declared as enforceable, most importantly the provision requiring Bob to work the full year. Bob would still be able to raise all of the other issues mentioned in this essay, in his response to a Complaint for Declaratory Relief.

Plaintiff, Bob's Response to Defenses

<u>Merger Clause</u>
- The fact pattern does not mention whether the contract contains a <u>Merger clause</u>, a standard provision which states that the contract language is final, and that all prior drafts and oral agreements "merge" into this document. Thus, if Bob has a prior contract draft which indicates a favorable

interpretation or explanation of the one year stipulation, then he might be able to introduce this evidence at trial. However, that would be assuming facts outside the fact pattern, and Defendants would still argue that the final agreement was unambiguous under the <u>Parole Evidence Rule</u>.

Conclusions

1- Bob will likely lose his Breach of Contract claim.
2- Bob may prevail on his Equity claim for Quantum Meruit. (with the amount of damages determined by the judge)
3- The fact pattern does not provide enough information to assess the merits of the Equity claim for Promissory Estoppel, or for the Defendants' defenses.
4- The Cast and Producers could file a Complaint for Declarative Relief for a judge's interpretation of the contract.
5- The one year stipulation is unambiguous and thus Bob may have difficulty getting around the parol evidence rule.

Appendix E

Books that Motivate Professor Binder

The following books motivate me for different reasons, whether it's a book's message, humor, or carefully crafted words:

A People's History of the United States by Howard Zinn – A historical perspective written about those who never get to write the history books.

Biographies: *Ted Williams* by Leigh Monteville & *Rod Serling* by Joel Engel – I love reading biographies of people who are no longer alive, so you get a glimpse of their vibrancy in youth and the fragility of life toward the end.

Bonfire of the Vanities by Tom Wolfe - The best written book I've ever read.

Bright Lights Big City by Jay McInerney- A wild and dizzying novel written from the hip.

Fire in the Streets: America in the 1960's by Milton Viorst – This book discusses a lot of the volatile issues facing America in a turbulent decade.

Essentials of Screenwriting by Richard Walter, *Four Screenplays* by Syd Field, and *How to Write a Screenplay in 21 Days* by Vicky King – Any writer can learn a lot about structure from these books on the screenwriting process.

Heaven is a Playground by Rick Telander – The best sports book ever written.

On Writing by Stephen King – The word master offers a memoir with insights into his writing madness.

The Birthmark by Nathaniel Hawthorne – A short story which reminds readers to appreciate what they've got, and not obsess over trying to make a good thing perfect.

The Buffalo Creek Disaster by Gerald Stern – An excellent book which details a lawyer's effort to hold a mining company accountable for the deaths of several miners and family members. This book does not offer the fast-paced Hollywood glamorized version of a law case. Instead, the reader learns about how slow the litigation process can be.

The Fifties by David Halberstam – This 800-plus page book provides parallels between United States politics in the 1950's and politics near the turn of the century.

The Pre-Historic History of the Far Side by Gary Larsen – Larsen, a legendary cartoonist, adds commentary about his cartoons in the funniest book I have ever read.

"Did You Know" Footnotes

Motivator #3 - Did You Know... The U.S. Bureau of Labor Statistics has not attempted to estimate the number of times people change careers in the course of their working lives. However, in September 2010, the Bureau found that from age 18 to age 44, individuals held an average of 11 jobs. See www.bls.gov/news.release/pdf/nlsoy.pdf.

Motivator #6 - Did You Know... In a 2007 survey of 800 attorneys, only 55 percent reported being satisfied with their career. "Pulse of the Legal Profession," *ABA Journal*, by Stephanie Francis Ward (October 1, 2007) http://www.abajournal.com/magazine/article/pulse_of_the_legal_profession.

Motivator #15 - Did You Know... The U.S. Bureau of Labor Statistics lists occupations with the largest job growth projected through the year 2018, starting with registered nurse. For the complete list: http://www.bls.gov/emp/ep_table_104.htm.

Motivator #22 - Did You Know... In 2011, the Federal Trade Commission approved the practice of employers conducting social media background checks going back seven years for job applicants. See "Feds Okay Start-up That Monitors Employees' Internet and Social Media Footprints," *Forbes*, by Kashmir Hill (June 15, 2011) http://www.forbes.com/sites/kashmirhill/2011/06/15/start-up-that-monitors-employees-internet-and-social-media-footprints-gets-gov-approval.

Motivator #25 - Did You Know... While it is true that the founder of FedEx did pitch his business plan in a college class, it is not true that the professor declared the idea as "unworkable" or that the student received a "C" on the paper. See http://www.snopes.com/business/origins/fedex.asp.

Motivator #68 - A National Institutes of Health study suggests that the region of the brain that inhibits risky behavior is not fully formed until age 25. The "still-developing brain areas govern judgment, decision-making and impulse control." See "Risky Business: Dealing with Your Teen's Behavior," NIH News in Health newsletter (September 2011) http://newsinhealth.nih.gov/issue/sep2011/feature1.

Motivator #98 - See the Mappiness Project at http://www.mappiness.org.uk.

Acknowledgements

Remembering that "the best writing is re-writing," (Motivator #61) I always turn to my inner circle (Motivator #33) for editing advice. I am eternally grateful to Bridget Binder, Dave Binder, Jody Blanke, Jill Brubaker, Julia Goodman, and Greg Henley. I am also a big believer in learning from my students (*Learn from your Learners*, the second "L" in L.I.G.H.T. B.U.L.B. Moments), and thank Ari Edlin and Sarah Homsi for their valuable input on the book.

About the Author

Perry Binder, J.D. teaches business law courses at Georgia State University, and blogs for the College section of *The Huffington Post*. His unique teaching style was crafted from years spent in hilarious classrooms and frenzied courtrooms, and from his belief that humor and self-awareness are the key ingredients for effective learning.

Perry received the Robinson College of Business Service Excellence and Teaching Excellence Awards in 2011 and 2005 respectively, and in 2008, he received the MBA Crystal Apple Teaching Award. Years earlier, he litigated complex business cases in Miami, and received the Dade County Bar Association's Pro Bono Award, for service to individuals unable to afford legal counsel.

Perry is a member of the National Speakers Association and a former radio talk show host who frequently appears in the media, including *USA Today, The New York Times, The Atlanta Journal Constitution, Associated Press, The Financial Times, CBS Radio, Court TV Radio,* and *ESPN Classic.*

For more information, please visit: **99Motivators.com**